W9-BYJ-663

CONTENTS

Published by ABDO Publishing Company, PO Box 398166, Minneapolis, MN 55439. Copyright © 2014 by Abdo Consulting Group, Inc. International copyrights reserved in all countries. No part of this book may be reproduced in any form without written permission from the publisher. The Core Library™ is a trademark and logo of ABDO Publishing Company.

Printed in the United States of America,
North Mankato, Minnesota
042013
092013

Editor: Blythe Hurley
Series Designer: Becky Daum

Library of Congress Control Number: 2013931970

Cataloging-in-Publication Data
Weil, Ann.
 Australia / Ann Weil.
   p. cm. -- (Continents)
ISBN 978-1-61783-931-3 (lib. bdg.)
ISBN 978-1-61783-996-2 (pbk.)
1. Australia--Juvenile literature.   I. Title.
919--dc23

                                                2013931970

Photo Credits: Dan Breckwoldt/Shutterstock Images, cover, 1, 36; Red Line Editorial, Inc., 4, 18; Shutterstock Images, 6, 10, 12, 17, 20, 23, 29, 43 (bottom), 45; Greg Ward NZ/Shutterstock Images, 9, 34; Keith Wheatley/Shutterstock Images, 14; Ian Scott/Shutterstock Images, 24, 42 (bottom); Dmitri Ogleznev/Shutterstock Images, 27; North Wind/North Wind Picture Archives, 30; Andrew Brownbill/AP Images, 32; Jan Kratochvila/Shutterstock Images, 41, 42 (middle); Janelle Lugge/Shutterstock Images, 42 (top); Meister Photos/Shutterstock Images , 43 (top); Andrzej Gibasiewicz/Shutterstock Images, 43 (middle)

CONTINENTS

AUSTRALIA

by Ann Weil

Content Consultant
Gregory S. Brown, PhD
Center for Australian and
New Zealand Studies
Georgetown University

CORE
LIBRARY

QUICK FACTS ABOUT AUSTRALIA

- **Highest point:** Mount Kosciuszko, 7,310 feet (2,228 m)

- **Area:** 2,988,902 square miles (7,741,220 sq km)

- **Distance north to south:** 2,291 miles (3,687 km)

- **Distance east to west:** 2,486 miles (4,000 km)

- **Key industries:** Finance, metals and mining, energy and utilities, industrial materials, health care and pharmaceuticals

- **Population:** 22,015,600

- **Five biggest cities:** Sydney, Melbourne, Brisbane, Perth, Adelaide

- **Most common languages:** English, Italian, Greek, Arabic, Cantonese, and Mandarin

WELCOME TO AUSTRALIA

Australia is the smallest continent on our planet. It is also the driest inhabited continent. (Only Antarctica is drier.) But while it may be the smallest continent, Australia is the largest island in the world.

Australia is a continent, an island, and a country. It is the sixth largest country in the world.

The Flinders Ranges mountains are found in southern Australia.

Oceania

Oceania is a region in the South Pacific Ocean that includes 14 countries. Some people consider these areas to be part of the same continent as Australia. One of these countries is New Zealand, Australia's neighbor to the southeast. New Zealand is one of the most beautiful and least populated countries in the world. In 1893 it became the first country in the world to give women the right to vote. Fiji, another Oceanian nation, is made up of 333 separate islands.

Ancient Australia

The land that is now Australia was once part of a huge, ancient landmass called Gondwana. Gondwana included what later became Australia, Antarctica, Africa, and India. Over millions of years, big chunks of Gondwana split off. This land broke apart into smaller, separate continents. Australia and Antarctica broke off together. Then, much later, Australia split from Antarctica and became its own continent.

Australia became isolated. So did whatever was living there at that time. Amazingly, some plants

An Aboriginal man plays a musical instrument called a didgeridoo.

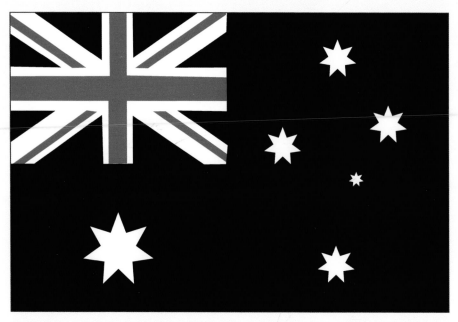

The Flag of Australia and the Southern Cross

A nation's flag includes symbols that are important to the people of that country. The Australian flag has the British flag (called the Union Jack) in its top left corner. The big star under the Union Jack is called the Commonwealth Star. It represents the six states of Australia and the territories. The other stars on the flag show a constellation called the Southern Cross. The Southern Cross is one of the most recognizable constellations in the Southern Hemisphere. What does looking at this flag tell you about the things that Australians believe make their country special?

and animals from the time of Gondwana still live in Australia. Scientists consider these species to be living fossils.

Who Lives in Australia?

People from Europe began to settle Australia during the late 1700s. But the first Australians were not from Europe. Aborigines, the native people of Australia, were living on this island long before Europeans arrived.

Much of Australia is too hot and dry for most people to live. There are a few Aboriginal communities in Australia's desert-filled middle. But there is not enough water in the outback for many homes or farms. Almost all Australians live in big cities close to the ocean.

Land of Fossils

Australia was not always so dry. Long ago, an

The Great Barrier Reef

One of Australia's most famous natural features, the Great Barrier Reef, is actually made out of tiny animals called coral. Coral reefs look like colorful rocks. But they are actually the bodies of small living things. The Great Barrier Reef is the largest natural feature on Earth. It is so big, astronauts in orbit around our planet can see it!

Koalas are among the many marsupials that call Australia home.

inland sea covered large parts of what is now the state of Queensland and central Australia. Over time that water evaporated, but the sea left its mark on the land. The remains of ancient ocean animals were preserved as fossils. Now this part of Australia is a rich source of dinosaur fossils. Today, people around the world are fascinated by Australia's curious animals, such as the kangaroo, koala, and platypus.

EXPLORE ONLINE

Chapter One talked about Australia's prehistoric history and Aboriginal people. The Web site below focuses on the same subjects. As you know, every source is different. How is the information given on this Web site different from the information in this chapter? What can you learn from this Web site?

Prehistoric Australia
www.mycorelibrary.com/australia

CHAPTER TWO

THE LAND OF AUSTRALIA

Australia is low and flat. In fact, at only a little above sea level, it is the lowest of all the continents. Its average elevation is 1,082 feet (330 m). That's not even as tall as many skyscrapers. But Australia does have some mountains.

Australia is also the driest populated continent. However, it does rain in Australia. The northeastern part of Australia in particular gets heavy rainfall.

The orange and black striped sandstone domes of the Bungle Bungle Mountain Range in Western Australia are shaped like beehives.

Uluru

Uluru, which Australians also call Ayers Rock, is a large rock formation in central Australia. It is 1,142 feet (348 m) tall and 5.8 miles (9.3 km) around. Uluru is one of the nation's most recognizable landmarks. Tourists come to see this giant rock appearing to glow red at sunrise and sunset. The area around Uluru is home to springs, rock caves, and ancient paintings. Like many other natural features in Australia, Uluru is sacred to the Aboriginal people.

There are jungles and rain forests in that part of the continent.

The Great Dividing Range

The tallest mountain in Australia is Mount Kosciuszko, which is 7,310 feet (2,228 m) high. Mount Kosciuszko is part of the Great Dividing Range, home of Australia's highest peaks. The country's longest rivers are also a part of this mountainous region. The Great Dividing Range separates the east coast of Australia from the rest of the continent. It affects the weather, as well as how and where people live and farm.

Uluru, also called Ayers Rock, is among Australia's most recognizable landmarks.

Compared with the rest of Australia, the Great Dividing Range has high rainfall and humidity levels. It also has a wet and a dry season. During the wet season, it sometimes rains as much as 19 days a month.

The Murray-Darling River Basin

The Murray-Darling River Basin is Australia's longest continuous river system. This area receives very little rainfall. But it is still an important water source

Equatorial
Tropical
Subtropical
Desert
Grassland
Temperate

Australia's Climate Zones

Australia's Climate Zones and Population Density

This map shows the different climate zones in Australia. It also shows the most important cities in Australia. As you look at the map, think about why people live in certain parts of the country. Where do most people live in Australia? Why do you think this is so?

for the people of Australia. People use this water for irrigating crops, drinking, bathing, and many other things.

The Australian government made the Murray-Darling basin even better for farmers by building dams and waterways there. As a result, this area has become a major food-growing region known as "Australia's food bowl." It covers more than 621,371 square miles (1,609,344 sq km) in southeastern Australia.

Tasmania

The country of Australia includes islands as well as the mainland. Tasmania is a large island state off the southeast coast of the mainland. Unlike the rest of Australia, Tasmania has a cool climate. In fact, in winter, this island even has snow!

Kati Thanda–Lake Eyre

Kati Thanda–Lake Eyre is a large salt lake in one of the driest regions of central Australia. The average rainfall in this area is only four to six inches (10 to 15 cm) a year. This lake is almost always dry. However, it is filled by floodwater about every three years. When this happens, it becomes the largest lake in Australia and the eighteenth largest in the world. At these times it also becomes the temporary home of several species of fish.

CHAPTER THREE

KANGAROOS, KOALAS, AND MORE

Because of its isolation, Australia is home to plants and animals found nowhere else on Earth.

Many of Australia's unusual animals, such as kangaroos and koalas, are marsupials. Like other mammals, female marsupials give birth to live babies and nurse their young. But marsupial babies are born when they are much younger than other mammals.

Kangaroos are among Australia's many marsupial mammals.

Tiny and blind marsupial babies crawl into their mothers' pouches to nurse soon after birth. There they are safe until they can survive in the outside world.

Although people call them bears, koalas are really marsupials like kangaroos. Koalas are picky eaters. They feed only on leaves from a few kinds of eucalyptus trees.

There are many other Australian marsupials, including bandicoots, wombats, and Tasmanian devils.

The saltwater crocodile, which Australians call the salty,

Venomous Animals of Australia

Australia is home to many venomous, or poisonous, animals. Venomous Australian animals include snakes, the platypus, spiders, scorpions, octopuses, jellyfish, mollusks, stonefish, and stingrays. The platypus is a member of the animal family known as monotremes. Monotremes are the only mammals that lay eggs. Platypuses have a bill much like a duck's and webbed feet. Male platypuses have spurs on their hind feet that contain venom strong enough to be extremely painful to humans.

"Salties," or saltwater crocodiles, can weigh almost as much as a car.

is the largest crocodile species in the world. Salties can reach up to 23 feet (7 m) long and weigh more than 2,205 pounds (1,000 kg). They can be very dangerous to people. They live both on the coast and in northern Australia's freshwater rivers and wetlands.

The Australian bird known as the kookaburra makes a cackling noise that sounds like laughter. Their calls are sometimes loud enough to wake up a whole neighborhood in the morning. People throughout the world are familiar with these birds because of a popular Australian nursery rhyme written in 1932.

Australia's Great Barrier Reef is home to an astonishing number of marine animals.

Marine Life

The Great Barrier Reef is the world's largest coral reef system. Coral reefs look like colorful rocks. But they are actually the bodies of small living things called coral. The Great Barrier Reef is the largest natural feature on Earth. Whales, dolphins, sea turtles, sea snakes, and more than 1,500 species of fish live there. So does the unusual sea mammal called the dugong. These animals are similar to manatees.

James Cook, who lived from 1728 to 1779, was a British explorer. He discovered Australia in June 1770. The following text is from his journal entry regarding his sighting of a kangaroo:

> *As I was walking this morning at a little distance from the ship, I saw myself one of the animals which had been so often described; it was of a light mouse-colour, and in size and shape very much resembling a greyhound; it had a long tail also, which it carried like a greyhound; and I should have taken it for a wild-dog, if, instead of running, it had not leapt like a hare or deer: Its legs were said to be very slender, and the print of its foot to be like that of a goat; but where I saw it the grass was so high that the legs were concealed, and the ground was too hard to receive the track.*

> Source: Robert Kerr. *"SECTION XXXI."* The Project Gutenberg EBook of *A General History and Collection of Voyages and Travels*, Vol. 13. *Project Gutenberg. Web. Accessed February 2, 2013.*

Consider Your Audience

Read the passage above closely. How could you adapt Cook's words for a modern audience, such as your neighbors or your classmates? Write a blog post giving this same information to the new audience. What is the most effective way to get your point across to this audience? How is the language you use for your new audience different from Cook's original text? Why?

CHAPTER FOUR

THE PEOPLE OF AUSTRALIA

People have been living in Australia for at least 40,000 years. The ancestors of Australia's native people came from Southeast Asia. They traveled to Australia by sea. These first Australians were hunter-gatherers. This means they hunted animals for meat and gathered what food they could from the natural world around them. They also traded with other peoples in Oceania and Asia. They

Australia's ancient people left behind images depicting their culture and beliefs.

Boomerangs

Some Aboriginal people used a weapon called a boomerang to hunt. Boomerangs are curved, flat pieces of wood. They were ideal for hunting kangaroo and large, flightless birds called emu. Some boomerangs were able to return to the thrower after being thrown. But many did not. Boomerangs that did not return were usually bigger, heavier, and more powerful. Boomerangs are now a popular souvenir for tourists.

did not build cities or have a written language. But they did have a rich culture. They expressed themselves through stories, art, and music.

By the time people from Europe arrived to explore Australia, there were between 300,000 and 1 million Aboriginal people living throughout the continent. They lived in groups called tribes.

Dreamtime

Aboriginal people share a belief in the Dreamtime or Dreaming. Their stories tell of a time long ago, known as the Dreamtime, when ancestor spirits created the world. The ancestor spirits then turned into natural objects. Aboriginal people believe their ancestor

Boomerangs painted with Aboriginal-style designs are a common souvenir of a trip to Australia.

spirits continue to live inside rocks and other things in nature.

European explorers who came to Australia did not believe they were taking Australia from the Aboriginal people. British explorer James Cook claimed Australia for Great Britain in 1770. In 1788, the British established their first Australian colony on land that is now part of the city of Sydney. The first European settlers were mostly convicts and their jailers. British jails were overcrowded, and the British government needed a new place to send these people.

Australia's population grew rapidly when prospectors flooded the country hoping to find gold during the 1850s.

After the arrival of the British, European illnesses killed many Aborigines. Because they had never been exposed to these diseases, the Aborigines did not have immunity. Immunity is the ability to resist a disease or illness. European settlers eager to create farmland also drove many Aborigines out of their homelands.

The Australian Gold Rush

Gold was discovered in Australia in 1851. A gold rush soon followed. The population exploded as people from all over the world flocked to Australia. More than 700,000 immigrants came to Australia between 1850 and 1860. Many moved from place to place in search of gold. Australia was no longer a British jail. It was becoming very much a place of its own.

Australians Today

More than 22 million people live in Australia today. Many Australians were born in other countries. People move there because of the high quality of life. Children receive a good education. Almost every Australian man and woman can read and write.

Today, descendants of the first Australians make up less than 3 percent of the country's population. Unlike most Australians, many live in poor communities and do not have access to good health care.

Australians enjoy the Melbourne Cup horse race as a place to show off their fashion sense.

Sports

Australians love both playing and watching sports. Australians play football, but they call it footy and have different rules from American football. Cricket is another popular Australian sport.

Since most Australians live in cities near the coast, getting to the beach is easy. Swimming and beach volleyball are popular ways to have fun.

The first Tuesday in November is the day of a popular horse race called the Melbourne Cup. This race is so important to Australians that it is a public holiday in the city of Melbourne.

Holidays

Australia's holidays reflect its unique history and customs. January 26 is a national holiday called Australia Day. People celebrate the day with parades, concerts, barbecues, and beach parties. This holiday began as a way to remember the landing of the first Europeans and the British colonization

Christmas in July

Australia is in the Southern Hemisphere. This means it is summer in Australia when people in North America and Europe are experiencing winter. Christmas comes at what is often the hottest time of the year. Many Australians celebrate that holiday by going to the beach or doing something else to cool off. Australians often celebrate Christmas again in July, when the weather is cooler. They enjoy this holiday in many of the same ways we do here in North America, exchanging gifts and eating a special meal with family.

A World War II veteran proudly displays his medals during ANZAC Day services in Auckland, New Zealand.

of the country. Now it is also an occasion to celebrate the country's cultural diversity.

Another important Australian holiday is called ANZAC Day. On April 25, Australians and New Zealanders hold dawn services to honor the lives of all Australians lost during wartime. This national holiday began in 1916, a year after thousands of Australian and New Zealander soldiers died in a bloody battle at Gallipoli, in Turkey, during World War I (1914–1918). These soldiers were called ANZACs, which is short for the Australian and New Zealand Army Corps.

When Australians voted to choose a new national anthem in 1974, a song called "Waltzing Matilda" by Banjo Paterson came in second. It became so popular Australians now consider it their unofficial anthem:

Oh there once was a swagman camped in the billabong
Under the shade of a Coolibah tree
And he sang as he looked at the old billy boiling
Who'll come a'waltzing Matilda with me . . .

Down came a jumbuck to drink at the billabong
Up jumped the swagman and grabbed him with glee
And he said as he put him away in the tucker bag
You'll come a'waltzing Matilda with me . . .

Source: Banjo Paterson. "Waltzing Matilda." *National Library of Australia.*
National Library of Australia, June 6, 2011. Web. Accessed February 15, 2013.

Back It Up

Take a close look at the lyrics of Paterson's song. They tell the story of a traveling worker, or "swagman," making some tea at a bush camp and capturing a sheep to eat. Using context clues, think about what some of the other unfamiliar words in this piece might mean. What evidence can you find to back up your ideas?

CHAPTER FIVE

AUSTRALIA TODAY AND TOMORROW

Australia is a democracy with an elected government. In fact, it is one of the oldest continuous democracies in the world. Unlike the United States, where people can choose whether or not they wish to vote, all Australian citizens over the age of 18 must vote in both federal and state elections.

Australia's Parliament House features a large mosaic designed by indigenous artist Michael Nelson Jagamara.

Australia's government is divided into three branches. Australia has an elected legislature, an executive branch headed by a prime minister who is also a member of the legislature, and a high court. The British king or queen is still the official head of state in Australia. But he or she does not take part in governing the country. Some Australians want the country to become a republic with a president as head of state. But Australians voted against a complete separation from Britain in 1999.

Australia is a wealthy country. Most people

Madame Prime Minister

Like the United States, Australia was first settled by the British. But unlike the United States, Australia did not fight the British for their independence. Queen Elizabeth II of Great Britain is also Queen of Australia. However, the Queen does not rule Australians. Australians elect legislators who then choose a prime minister to head their government. Australia's parliament appointed Julia Gillard as prime minister in 2010. She was the first woman to hold this office.

work in trade, businesses that serve the public, and manufacturing. Australia's manufactured goods include food, chemicals, and machinery. Australia has many natural resources, including oil, coal, and natural gas. Mines produce iron, copper, opals, and sapphires.

Although agriculture is only a small part of the country's economy, Australia is one of the world's largest producers of wool, which comes from more than 100 million Australian sheep. Farmers also grow wheat, vegetables, fruit, nuts, cotton, and other crops.

Living with Less Water

An unusually long dry spell is called a drought. During a drought, there is not enough water to meet people's needs. Drought is not a new problem in Australia. But with its population higher than ever, the demand for water is growing at the same time the supply is drying up. Less water means less produce, which means higher food prices in stores.

The Sydney Opera House

The Sydney Opera House is one of the most recognizable and beautiful buildings in the world. Designed by Danish architect Jørn Utzon, it cost about $102 million to build. It is among the busiest performing arts venues in the world, hosting more than 1,500 performances a year. Its roof weighs more than 161,000 tons.

Australians are trying new strategies to conserve water, including water restrictions. Water restrictions tell people how and when they can use water. For example, local governments can fine Australians for using sprinklers on their lawns.

Australia has problems to face in the future, including droughts and improving the lives of its Aboriginal people. But many people all over the world think of this special continent as a wonderful place to live, work, and visit. From its unique wildlife to its rich history, Australia is truly a land like no other!

The Sydney Opera House is recognized around the world as an architectural masterpiece.

FURTHER EVIDENCE

Chapter Five talked about Australia's growing water shortage and what the Australian people and government can do to combat the problem. If you could pick out the main point of this information, what would it be? What evidence did the author give to support that point? Visit the Web site below to learn more about Australia's water shortage. Choose a quote from the Web site that relates to this chapter. Does this quote support the author's main point? Does it make a new point? Write a few sentences explaining how the quote you found relates to this chapter.

Australia's Water Crisis
www.mycorelibrary.com/australia

Uluru (Ayers Rock)

Uluru rises 1,142 feet (348 m) from the Australian outback. This amazing rock formation appears to glow red at sunrise and sunset.

Uluru, also called Ayers Rock

Sydney Harbor

This area is home to two of Australia's most famous man-made structures, the Sydney Opera House and Sydney Harbor Bridge.

The Sydney Opera House and Sydney Harbor Bridge

The Great Barrier Reef

With approximately 3,000 individual reef systems, this is the world's largest coral reef. Scuba divers and snorkelers can get up close to many animals in this incredible habitat.

The Great Barrier Reef

A partially collapsed lava tube at Undara National Park

Limestone rock formations in the Pinnacles Desert in Western Australia

A frill-necked lizard in Kakadu National Park

Undara Lava Tubes

Millions of years ago, an active volcano spewed lava in far northern Queensland. Some of this lava crusted over and formed tubes. Today visitors can walk where lava once flowed.

Pinnacles Desert

Limestone rock formations rise from the sandy desert floor in this area near the coast of Western Australia. Some are as tall as 13 feet (4 m) high.

Kakadu National Park

Australia's Kakadu National Park is home to rare and endangered animals, some of which live nowhere else on Earth. Visitors can also see ancient rock art made by Aboriginal people.

STOP AND THINK

Another View

There are many sources online and in your library about Australia. Ask a librarian or another adult to help you find a reliable source on Australia. As you know, every source is different. Compare what you learn in this new source with what you found out in this book. Then write a short essay comparing and contrasting the new source's perspective on Australia with the ideas in this book. How are they different? How are they similar? Why do you think they are different or similar?

Take a Stand

This book discusses how the British sent convicts to Australia. British prisons were overcrowded. But did the British have the right to send people to a land where Aboriginal people already lived? Write a short essay explaining your opinion. Make sure to give reasons for your opinion, and facts and details that support those reasons.

Say What?

Learning about a different continent can mean learning a lot of new vocabulary. Find five words in this book that you've never heard before. Use a dictionary to find out what they mean. Then write the meanings in your own words. After that, try to use each word in a new sentence.

Surprise Me

The plants and animals found in Australia can be interesting and surprising. What two or three facts about Australian plants and animals did you find most surprising? Write a few sentences about each fact. Why did you find them surprising?

GLOSSARY

Aboriginal
of or relating to the indigenous peoples of Australia

colonization
the establishment of colonies; the act of colonizing

convict
a person found guilty of a criminal offense and serving a sentence of imprisonment

evaporate
to turn from liquid into vapor

hemisphere
a half of the earth, as divided into northern and southern halves by the equator

immigrant
a person who has left one country to live in another

irrigation
supplying dry land with water by means of dams, waterways, etc.

marsupial
a group of mammals in which the young are born in an immature state and continue development in the mother's pouch

monotreme
a primitive group of mammals that lay eggs

sea level
the level of the ocean's surface, used to determine land heights and sea depths

venomous
secreting or capable of injecting venom by means of a bite or sting

LEARN MORE

Books

Arnold, Caroline. *Uluru: Australia's Aboriginal Heart*. New York: Clarion Books, 2003.

Berkes, Marianne. *Over in Australia: Amazing Animals Down Under*. Nevada City, CA: Dawn Publications, 2011.

Friedman, Mel. *Australia and Oceania*. New York: Scholastic, 2009.

Web Links

To learn more about Australia, visit ABDO Publishing Company online at **www.abdopublishing.com**. Web sites about Australia are featured on our Book Links page. These links are routinely monitored and updated to provide the most current information available.

Visit **www.mycorelibrary.com** for free additional tools for teachers and students.

INDEX

ABOUT THE AUTHOR

Ann Weil is the author of many books for children. She grew up in New York City and began her career in publishing there after college. Weil spent several years "Down Under" in New Zealand and Australia. She now lives in New Hampshire.